# Pigeons

*poems*
## Lois Rosen

Traprock Books • Eugene, Oregon
2004

Grateful acknowledgment is made to the following
publications in which these poems, some in slightly
different forms, first appeared:

*Calapooya Collage*  An Afternoon When It Might Clear
*Calyx*  Pigeons
*Clark College Writing Awards*  Davidson's Quarry
*Fireweed*  Blizzard II, How to Swallow Grief,
  The Living Language, My Bronx
*Five Fingers Review*  Ancestor Worship
*Graffiti Rag*  Webcrawler
*Heliotrope*  Terrelli's Peaches, The Hoyer Lift,
  What the Fish Asked
*The Homestead Review*  Lauren Bacall
*Hubbub*  Loew's Paradise, Snow Angels
*Jefferson Monthly*  Potato in Both Worlds
*Northwest Magazine*  Pumpkin Carving
*Northwest Review*  Sweet Potato
*Sow's Ear Poetry Review*  Widow
*Willow Springs*  How to Play Wedding, Blizzard
*Writer's Forum*  This Passover, Survivor

**PIGEONS** is published in a second edition of 300
and sold by independent bookstores in Oregon.

Traprock Books
1330 East 25th Avenue
Eugene, Oregon 97403

Cover illustration and inside art: Sally Brodigan.
Author Photo: Susanlee Graves.
Book design: Herb Everett, Peace Rose Graphics.
Printed on 60# Vanguard EcoBlend from Living Tree Paper.

ISBN 0-9714945-6-8

# CONTENTS

**IV**

The ⤸ symbol at the bottom
of a right-hand page indicates
the poem continues.

*In loving memory of my mother and father,*

*Nettie Miriam Liebowitz*
*and*
*Nathan Michael Liebowitz*

I

# MY BRONX

*for Else Odza*

I am going back in July
to the beautiful leafy Bronx
the hidden section beside the Hudson
where bus lines don't go
where Else and I stroll
lanes with no sidewalks
where she carries nail scissors
snips a roadside bouquet
of Queen Anne's lace.
Passing each mansion, she updates me
on which ambassadors live there now
the latest scandals.

At Wave Hill, the public park
no signs point to, where boomboxes
athletic gear and outside food are forbidden,
where sweeping lawns befit the legendary inhabitants
Twain and Toscanini, a landscape artist
of international renown
maintains the English garden, the reflecting pool.
Park of painters, readers, and writers at work
right here in the Bronx.  I'm not kidding.

This is the Bronx of my young heart,
my beautiful Bronx thirty years ago,
where Eileen Ruzow's father takes us
cruising on the river,
where the wind tousles my hair
and I am Venus, breaking hearts,
giggling, sipping ginger ale.

The road I walk with Else
is the same lover's lane where a boy and I
parked his parents' sixties Oldsmobile
when we went to college but lived at home.
Here under maples we belonged lip to lip.

When I visit Else now on the balcony
of her apartment eight stories above the river,
we retell our history, milestones of the year.
She tells me the pike return
as the Hudson becomes cleaner.
Her terrace is a bower of
windowbox impatiens pale as mist.
The moonflower flings open its rare blossom,
a huge morning glory
that blooms at night and smells like
lifelong friendship would if it were perfume.
The bridge to New Jersey shines in the darkness.

## SNOW ANGELS

Early snow was best
before the plow came
before Louis the Super
crooned "Chattanooga Choochoo"
to the clang of the shovel.
Yonkers, our Bride of
Winter cloaked in ermine,
and didn't we feel rich
everything clean and gleaming?

I sang *Frosty the Snowman*
*was a jolly, happy soul.*
My blanket shifted like
a snowdrift. *Gae shlufen!*
*Shh*! *Go back to bed!*
Do you want to wake
your father?

No matter.
I read *The Bobbsey Twins*
*at the Ice Carnival*
with the radiolight
Uncle Sam Berkowitz
had rigged above my bed
the blanket hugging
my body although
it was years too early
to even consider my body
a body.

While everyone slept
our souls flew
right to God singing.
Angels had feathers
softer than snow,
voices more beautiful
than Rosemary Clooney's.

Quiet didn't exist
in Heaven.
Nobody's mother yelled,
*Quiet, you'll wake the dead!*
Grandpa sang "*Hava Nageela*"
with God
and the snow angels danced
as early as they wanted.

# LOEW'S PARADISE

My parents take me to *West Side Story*.
Under my dotted swiss with the peter pan collar,
I wear a real bra–thirty two double A.  Linda Morris
doesn't even get her period.

At the candy counter, I choose Coke and Jujubes.
An usher in a tuxedo leads us down the rose carpet.
His white glove points where to sit.
Soon, I am pretty Maria in the bridal shop.

But a hand reaches around the seat, grabs my breast.
On the aisle side, Dad and Mom don't see, a big, dirty hand.
Robert Perozio in my class has really dirty hands.
Mrs. Cooper screams and makes him stay inside at recess.
Candy Spitalnik whispers that Robert's mother drinks.
My parents say when someone is drunk, stay away.
No telling what they will do.  They act crazy.

My breast is a tiny twig inside a bonfire.
I can't scream. If you see a criminal's face
he has to kill you.  Father never exercises.
He could have a heart attack.  It would be my fault.
No one will believe me.  Mother always says, *See.*
*There's nothing to be afraid of.*

I dump my drink on the hand.
Fingers let go.  Cold soda soaks my dress.
I see Coke stains in the lobby mirror.
*She's burning up.  Maybe we better take her right home.*
*Such a shame.  You waited so long for this.*
I turn my face from the candy seller's red uniform,
fake gold epaulets, the awful smell of popcorn.

# CONEY ISLAND

I wish I were still riding the El taking an entire
seventh grade class to Coney Island:
Little Ana, Lily Carbonell, Vivian Pantoja
who lived up the urine-stinking flights of
housing project stairs, triple-locked inside.

They waded in the tepid ocean, holding hands,
the Atlantic up to their shoulders, and jumped
as the waves broke, drenching everyone:
Victor, Angel, Marisol, who got pregnant in
the eighth grade, but this was one year earlier
when kicking just meant splashing games,
a long train ride away from St. Ann's Avenue.

In the clattering car back to the Bronx,
it didn't matter if Carmelo or Dora's hand sped
down the silver pole or who bumped who
as the teetery motion slid their wet towels
flying off Maria Polanco's lap. Terrible humidity,
staring commuters, screeching brakes:
nothing prevented us that afternoon
from laughing on that high track.

# THE LIVING LANGUAGE

As we hike
from summer camp
the city
is another country
ashes of an old world
whose language
we refuse to speak.
Far behind us
that ancient
European march
that bloody marching.

*Guttenyu.*
*Sha*!
Dead words
may they rest
in peace   those
old-fashioned coats
reaching the ground
those captives
outnumbering
the guards
but compliant
rounded up
shaved bald
naked.

No.  No more chattering
in the crematoria.
We'll rest
awhile   eat
baloney sandwiches
our apples
our Hershey bars

15

and drink
from canteens
doze in the
good green grass
of New York State
then continue along
singing "Open Road"
and "Zum Galli Galli"
English or Hebrew songs.

We return to camp
for free swim   dinner
and lights out
clean sheets
and our fathers'
army blankets
saved from
World War II
tucking us in.

# SWAN MAIDEN

Campfire coals glow under our marshmallows.
Yonkers girls, rosy-faced in firelight:
we don't need stoves, silverware, parents, or boys.
We turn sticks we've stripped with our own penknives,
brown marshmallows without burning, an art.

Holding a knife, let alone an ax,
a small miracle, no mother scolding,
*You'll cut yourself, poke someone's eye out.*
*Don't eat that marshmallow.*
*It's traif,* unkosher.

I'm here smelling the Prell we shampoo with
right in the lake. Frogs and crickets serenade
as I surface dive, tumble underwater,
breaststroke, flutterkick to Tchaikovsky,
water beads glittering on my wings.

# SURVIVOR

Camp Yonkers was not
the Yonkers where we
triple-locked doors
squinted through peepholes.
Safe sleep meaning every inch
of blanket tucked under
and Toby Kaufman's parents
had numbers tattooed
on their forearms,
numbers we could see
every time they reached
to hug us, while parents
kept hammering *Don't trust
anyone who isn't Jewish.*
Funny Mrs. Cooper,
beloved Mrs. Casecci–
in a pinch, would they
have lined us up,
the Jewish kids?
Aunt Francie who tucked
shiny quarters inside our
Halloween candy, Mrs. Lustrati
and her caramel apples–
if ordered to, would they
have substituted
cyanide for sugar?

I loved sleeping out
summer nights on the grass,
every twig and rock poking me.
Bug bitten but no matter.
Rima of the Emerald Forest
didn't need a roof, a bed.
I could find kindling,
roast my own hotdog, knew
which snakes were garters
and let them slither up
my arms, their blood
the temperature of my body,
their neon stripes dry
against my skin.  I could
identify copperheads
and rattlers, remember
the lessons about survival:
cut a deep x in my arm,
suck the venom, and always
always spit it out.

# HOW TO PLAY WEDDING

Under the veil
Mona keeps weeping
like during *Queen for a Day*
when the prize may be
a new Maytag.

If only she could whisper
she needs a Kleenex.
Thank God
her mother sewed in
dress shields.

Her friend married at an estate
beneath a trellis of roses.
Mona gets waxy gladioli
at the Bronxview Bridal Palace
under the El.

June, just after Mantle
rounded the bases
and was crossing home,
Richard slipped a diamond
on her finger.

One look at the *Vogue* gown
and her mother said,
*Ridiculous* and *Watch!*
*If you have sex with him,*
*he won't marry you,*

but the rabbi is chanting.
The crowd reads, stands up,
sits down, stands, sits.
Richard stomps the wine glass
beneath his heel.

Boom, her mother collapses.
Aunt Bessie, Aunt Selma,
the whole contingent
of second cousins
slumps to the floor.

*Wait. A wedding ceremony*
*must not be interrupted.*
Didn't Mona's mother warn her
not to marry young?
Now Mona's killed her.

The caterer's fuming,
but the couple runs into
The Versailles Room unannounced:
Mr. and Mrs. Richard Klein.
It was dizziness, hot lights.

Mona will be dumping her dress
at the Salvation Army
while the flower girl
is showing her friends
how to play wedding:

It's really easy.
Just fall down.

# BRIDGE BETWEEN TENSES

I don't know what I stumbled on,
a root, a stump, my own feet—
maple bark sharp
against my cheek,
blood gushing from my mouth.

The next day, Dr. Lefrak wept.
Years of braces wasted.
*How stupid can you be*, Mother said.
It was moot.  After all,
I'm the one

who ran into a tree,
knocked out my front teeth
and swallowed one.
But who wouldn't sob
on the phone at summer camp

hearing that an old boyfriend,
his freckled face, his chubby body—
smashed through a windshield.
New Guinea tribeswomen cut off
a finger each time someone dies.

But maiming?
A nice agnostic Jewish girl
in 1965?  The boyfriend survived,
became a doctor.
When I broke up with him

Mother warned, *You're trading*
*diamonds for garbage,*
but I had Grandma's diamonds
made into cufflinks
for my future ex-husband.

Now off-white porcelain
fools people, and my tongue
adjusts to the taste of metal.
A shame, but you get used to it–
car accidents, divorces.

Mother would say,
*Your fresh mouth*
*will get you in trouble.*
Now I can't tell
if I'm laughing
or crying.
What innocent things
will be broken in my path?

# TERRELLI'S PEACHES

*For Kevin*

We never ate those peaches
walled in behind a wooden fence,
tips of trees loaded with ripened globes–
red and golden, tantalizing kids who
could almost taste the sugary pulp,
lick the nectar cooling their chins.

On a block of working class Jews,
the name Terrelli stood for everything Italian:
*pallazos, contessas, ravioli, tortoni,*
*Michelangelo* painting suspended in air,
*That's Amore, Three Coins in a Fountain*
where wishes are granted in Rome.

And always it is Love:
Audrey Hepburn.
The Prince disguised as a commoner
willing to sacrifice the villa, the title
for her, the princess we girls on
Elliott Avenue dream of becoming.

Someday Richard Cantor
will stop playing stick ball and notice me.
Someday, he'll beg for my hand.
I'll say, *Perhaps.  Bring me the ripest*
*peach from Terrelli's.*  No one we know
has ever scaled that fence.

When I grow up I will marry
a man like Terrelli who wraps
his trees in canvas every winter,
who will wrap his arms around me
leaving every branch unbroken,
ready to bloom.

# II

# FATHER ON EARTH

Loneliness clinging to the sidewalks
of Yonkers, the streetlights damping down.

Anyone's fanciful Jewish father
with drawstring sacks of wrinkled wash–

hodgepodge rainbows of blouses, boxers, socks,
pillows blocking the moon.

He limps from the littered curb to the parking lot
of gravel, found marbles, found dimes.

Graceful father with eyes
as blue and open as oceans, father

for all games in the arcade, someone to throw
the bullseye, someone to redeem the ticket.

He, inside his dented car, on earth,
loading laundry sack by sack

on the crumby leatherette back seat
with a friendly nudge for each, a joke

about the good leg, and Ivory Snow,
one full cup for a load.

# EAT

Don't stare at your father.
Chew normally.
Swallow.
Ignore his sputtery gulps,
his spitting.
Turn on the radio,
hum along.

Don't waste one dab
of the raspberry shooting
out the donut's sides.
See the mess
you've made.

Doesn't he bring you
the candy apples he can't have?
Eat.
Say it's delicious.

Never tell Mama you're scared,
the picture you have of high up
the Empire State Building,
the tiny nudge it would take
to push him off.

Suppose your whole world
is small doors opened
by the nickels he
hands you at the automat.
Doors that fold up,
empty compartments,
no sweet roll,
the last one
not replaced.

# WHAT THE FISH ASKED

Fishing with my father on the pier, Yonkers,
slovenly stepsister of the city, squatted north
along the river. It was a good year when nothing
was wrong. Father was well, and we loved
our city. Any stinky brown water would do
because even in Yonkers, a fish could leap
from the river and grant us, shoulder to shoulder,
our wishes. He lowered his line farther,
red and white bakery string. It didn't
matter we used pencils instead of poles
because we fished far away from mother
and the city's lights.

The apple of his eye, whatever I did, I was
still his *sheina madel*, and once he'd been
a real soldier right across the river in Fort Dix,
when it really mattered, when Hitler's soldiers
could have bombed our city, and we,
especially all Jews, would have been dead,
not fishing. Certainly, there would be no
fishing, except for bloody bodies,
and even in Paris, they took Jewish fathers
and shot them. It didn't matter if they believed
in God or went to synagogue, the French rivers
went red and redder. *And what's the trouble,
little girl?* a fish asked. *You want to tell me
your wishes? Yes, keep my father healthy
forever, and don't let them burn New York City.*

# RIDING THE DUMBWAITER DOWN

With each new layer
of thick pink enamel gloss,
the kitchen closes in.
When Papa, Mama and the girl eat,
no one squeezes past.

The pilot light hisses
from the oven where a Jewish
child, a child her age
showers in the gas,
burns in the tales.

Red Riding Hood and the toothy wolf:
Grandma and the girl, two gallstones
in his gut.  Her stained little panties,
the Mama's girdle, the Papa's boxers,
dangling above their heads.

When will the terrible witch
remove her spell?
The child kisses and kisses
his mottled skin, but still
the prince is caught.

The Papa weighs ninety pounds,
and isn't this child the reason
he is living?  Even so, the gauze,
the ointment, the tape claw
at the wound.

Something rank exhales
inside those sacks of garbage
riding the dumbwaiter down.
Any child might lean over.
A push would do the trick.

She could be an orphan
in a packed train to Dachau
or maybe to England
with name and address
pinned to her jacket.

Yiddish songs recall the lost
ribbons, suitcases, cities.
The girl, the Mama, the Papa
take turns whipping egg whites
with a beater.

*Ze gu nisht helfen.* Nothing
helps. Spongecake
is not supposed to be
so hard or dry, but
they will eat it.

# THAT LAST TIME I SAW ARCHIE

*Veal saltimbucca, know what I mean?*
another transplanted New Yorker asked.
I nodded.  Who could forget marsala,
rosemary, meat rolls sauteed
in olive oil and butter
that last night after
I visited Uncle Archie
at Calvary Hospital in the Bronx
where he told the nun:
> *Born a Jew, lived as a Jew*
> *and when I meet my maker*
> *it'll be as a Jew.*

That day Aunt Henny brought soup,
still warm, and noodle pudding
he didn't thank her for.
But apologizing for the weakness
of his voice, frequently halting,
he retold stories about my father:
> *Oy, that Natie,*
> *what a character!  I'll never forget*
> *his beat up Chevrolet,*
> *the driver's side door tied on*
> *with rope.  The gang of us–*
> *Robbie Friedman, Squeaky Lazar.*
> *Your father tells us, "Get in*
> *and wait till the Texaco Hour begins."*
> *It always starts with a siren,*
> *and your crazy father*
> *rolls down all the windows*
> *and takes off down Carol Ave.*
> *ninety miles an hour.*

*Remember the one I told you*
*about him in Katz's deli?*
*After all, with those blue eyes,*
*everyone took him for Irish.*
*So the waiter says in Yiddish,*
*"Give him the old meat."*
*And didn't Natie in a perfect Yiddish*
*tell him a thing or two.*
*I almost split my sides.*

Exhausted afterwards, Henny and I wolfed
our food at "Patricia's Pizza & Pasta"
on Morris Avenue behind Calvary.
I hadn't eaten Italian bread that good
since I lived in the Bronx.
Minestrone with basil, plum tomatoes,
veal saltimbucca, spaghetti
swirled round our forks.

After dinner, past a playground
where a live band played "Stardust,"
my aunt, having dragged for months
to that hospital, twirled me
on the sidewalk in a foxtrot,
glided the two of us–slow
quick quick, slow quick quick–
into the twilight.

# PUMPKIN CARVING

### I
I stay in a hallway,
and my father lies
in an oxygen tent,
unconscious.

When they cut
cancer from
a face, food falls
from the mouth.

You use
a folded Kleenex
to cover parts
they remove.

### II
A candle leers yellow
in a grin,
thick hollow face,
insides blackening.

Carved,
they rot fast,
cave in like cheeks
sucked to a howl.

# BLIZZARD

*Snow fell on us like ashes.*
Elizabeth Rozner

Mona stands still before a curtain of snow,
a lace she cannot part.  She, the empty space
between each flake, something like air broken
and broken and broken. In a climate well below
freezing, how quickly Radford St. has disappeared.

This moment balances on the steps outside
Yonkers Professional Hospital, this box
around bodies, tortoise shell after the flesh
has washed away. One move forward will erase
all color, a lid lowering over the eye.

Do the eyes of the dead return to the blue
they were born with?  Her father had blue eyes.
People teased him, called him *Irish*. She can't
remember who closed those eyes, or if they were
closed already.  One night he drifted to sleep.

The next is this looking into blizzard nights
when snow covers everything, when they
bundle up and descend the staircase,
when she is a small figure between them
under the streetlamp, under the falling snow.

# III

# LAUREN BACALL

Nettie Berkowitz would be Lauren Bacall, cigarette
dangling, pageboy dipping seductively over one eye,
if she hadn't used permanents and peroxide,

if she weren't size eighteen,
if her father didn't own Berkowitz' Fountain and
hadn't kept commenting, *On you, it looks good.*

She'd be vacationing in Montauk with Frieda Katz,
all the girls from Klein's Jewelry on 47th Street,
if relatives weren't warning she'd be *an old maid.*

Nettie Liebowitz would have taken yearly vacations with
her husband to Miami if, six months later, there hadn't
been a pimple on his face that turned into carcinoma.

And then the miracle child they conceived despite radiation
turned out healthy but disdainful–and Nettie sees herself
in her daughter's eyes: a frizzy-haired, cigarette-breath Mom.

# WIDOW

Nettie enters
Jack's Appetizing Store
letting the door slam,
the horrid humidity of Jerome Ave.
behind her.

She bends toward the pickle barrels,
inhaling vinegars, garlic,
peppercorns floating in inky pools,
tubs brimming
with fingerlings, fatties,
tomatoes and peppers
soaking in brine,
one barrel for sour, one
for the extra sour,
the half and half,
the sweet.

*Here lady, you wanna taste?*
Such tartness
makes her eyes tear.
How can she help it?

Behind Jack's case:
the gold skin of the butterfish,
whole whitefish with glittering eyes,
carp—such pure white flesh—

and queen of them all,
the slab of belly lox reclining
like Cleopatra
on the wooden counter.

She takes her time
deciding, lingering
in front of the creamery butter,
an Empire State Building of spread,
as Jack's capable knife slices
for some housewife
who has to hurry home.

Not her. Not again.
Not ever.

# HOW TO SWALLOW GRIEF

Riding back in my car,
Aunt Henny and Aunt Katy weep.
They say I'm a good daughter, never that
I shouldn't have put their sister-in-law
away. When we arrive at my house,
Henny, seventy-six, with artificial knees
demonstrates dance routines she teaches
seniors. Let me inherit Henny's genes.

I beg the aunts for stories. Katy
says grandmother took bets, shoved
strips of paper in her brassiere
between her bosoms. Henny says,
*She didn't need to know that.*
My mother's parents rolled cigars, sold
*The Daily News* to men going home tired
after another shift at Otis Elevator.

In September, Henny phones from Yonkers
wishing Happy Rosh Hashonah.
New Year, my parents toasted with Mogen David,
*To a sweet new year.* Mother baked *taiglach*,
small balls of dough piled in pyramids
that honey dripped down.

Was it only four years ago
she began taping up words:
*phone, sofa, door?* She could still
answer my calls, count money,
say *Lois.*

## SWEET POTATO

Mother is alive.
She impales a sweet potato
with toothpicks, suspends it
in a glass.

*Oh, it's you!*

Gangly and tangled, vines leaf,
snake down shelves past glassware,
the kitchen sink, grope toward
the fire escape window. Roots
droop in foggy water.

November sunlight–a cold day.
In her right mind, Mother
wears a cardigan instead of baring
the back I scratch. *Good?* She
doesn't answer, lives in a room
she'll never find again.

All the same to her, I am more
of the nothing she can't name:
her old sofa, a dust mote,
a cloud.

# AN AFTERNOON WHEN IT MIGHT CLEAR

On a rainy afternoon
they call from the retirement home. *Please
take away her nail polish.
She's putting it on her face.*
They remind her to get dressed
so she puts slacks under her nightie.

When we get there I have to say,
*Take your fingers
out of your mouth, Mother.
Don't chew your napkin.
Yes, you do have a family.
This is David, your grandson.*

He sits next to me in the car.
When I was his age, she'd spank me.
She used to say,
*You think you're sad now?
Wait. I'll give you something
to cry about.*

# BLIZZARD II

Snow is spreading like that spidery lace tablecloth
my mother brought out on Passover when we pretended
we had a dining room, our dropleaf table expanded
into that living room where my parents slept.

Carrying the table into her retirement apartment, the movers
shiver. Frozen fog clings to greenery stiffened white.
Mother whines, *Where did that come from? I don't
want it.* She collapses on the couch sighing.

Forecasters warn of more snow, freezing rain.
In the nursing home her worldly goods
come to little drifts of clothes, costume jewelry,
one nightstand, glass birds.

This year a blizzard storms behind her eyes.
Until recently I would have said
*She knows me*, but now brakes won't grip.
The car ahead spins on ice as if demented.

# THE HOYER LIFT

Mother dangles from a diaper-shaped sling
midair, arms and legs akimbo,
her backside slumped into canvas.

No tilt-a-whirl squeals, her speech dwindled
into nothing from her two phrases for everything:
*hearing aid* and *one thirty-five*,
her apartment number before she began
knocking on doors after midnight,
burning holes in the carpet.

The nursing home allows smoking.
It wouldn't have mattered.
She stopped as if she'd forgotten
how to balance a Lucky Strike
between her yellowed knuckles.

It must have been like trying to lift
a hundred pound bar, this woman
who preferred walking
all the way to P.S. 13 every day,
who traveled to China and France.
Now hefty men strain their backs
trying to hoist her up,

so this mini-crane, The Hoyer Lift
elevates while the aides steady the chain.
*Get out of the way*, they say, politely.
Even from the hall, I hear machinery
groan as she plummets:
sad wingless bird.

# APPLE BLOSSOM

One afternoon six months ago, mother and I
sang in the nursing home corridor, our duet
drawing a cloak around us, and I guessed she recalled
what might have been her own mother's silk-lined alto.
Today apple trees blossom, dolled up for the funeral.

Her life contracted to one note, and mine opened
like white sheets on the line, each year's diminished
chords of bruised fruit
dropping crimson from the trees.

Her breathing slowed so gradually I held
her until the last, humming that song of
her youth, *Apple Blossom Time,* and kissing her cheek,
bending over as she used to do
to smooth the covers.  Hushed singer, mine
to hum and rock.

# THIS PASSOVER

*For Vera Joslow Bearg
and Randy Fishfader*

*Why is this night different
from all other nights?*
the child's prayer asks.
*Once we were slaves in Egypt,*
but these days we reuse
the old shankbone
Ronnie has kept in her freezer,
and the hard-boiled egg
the story says gets stronger
with boiling, cracks open.

Matzo, the bread, our foremothers
carried in the desert, the women
like the bread having no chance to rise,
and *maror*, the bitter herb
making our eyes tear without warning,
the way passing a woman
who resembles mother
can catch me in the throat–

and add to that the *charosis*,
diced apples, Manishevitz and cinnamon,
red brown like bricks.  Isn't this
the stinging sweetness of sacrifice,
the way mother kept sweating,
her applause and her yearning?

So you understand what it means
to have women at our seder
raise their glasses and say,
>  *Let's drink this wine*
>  *to Lois's mother.*
>  *Let's drink to Nettie.*

# PIGEONS

So am I going to interrupt
Mother's funeral
to argue with Cantor Gottlieb,
that same puffed up swallow
I've known since childhood
from The Sons of Israel?
Cantor twitters an apology.
Lacking a minyan of ten men,
mourner's *Kaddish* may not
be said at the grave.

Flocked near the mound
beside the pit
where Mother's been lowered,
Aunt Leah, Aunt Henny,
Aunt Nessy, the cousins
and I stand like doomed
passenger pigeons.
We don't exist.
After years in Oregon
where our rabbi
is a woman who cradles
torah scrolls in her arms,
I forgot the pecking order.

Cantor Gottlieb
proclaims Mother,
*Aishes heyel*,
"a woman of valor."
He means she ironed
every bit of clothing
including underwear
on humid summer nights.
He means she steamed
enough tongue and corned beef
to cater the whole
Jewish Veterans Club Dinner,
took the lists
my father handed her
and voted.

Cantor does not mean
the job she got,
so she would not always
ask for money.
He does not mean
times Father refused,
and Mother let me buy
a fancy graduation dress
at Genung's.

Cantor phones the evening
after the funeral to say
I can hire a devout,
impoverished old man
to say *Kaddish* for mother,
a woman he never knew,
if I pay, and after all
I do want to honor my mother,
don't I?

The telephone cord twists
around my fingers.
It's so easy
to strangle a bird.
Once, overseas,
I watched my hosts
troop to the dovecote,
lift a squab
and wring its neck,

but Mother didn't raise me
to screech *Vulture!*
*How dare you!* I peep,
*Thank you. That's been
taken care of.*
He repeats,
*You can't say Kaddish
for your mother.*

After so many years
in the balcony,
I can rock myself
to the melody: *Yis gadal
v'yis ka dash sh'may rabo ...*

# IV

# DAVIDSON'S QUARRY

That day   foxgloves
against the rock wall   spire
three feet tall   holding on

last blooms at the tips of stalks
lower ones turned to conical pods
not yet dry enough to burst

Odors of cow manure and mint
crushed leaves cupped to my face   inhaling
No noise from backhoes and scrapers

Stiff grass in the pond muck
it would be easy to slip
my husband warned me

He was at the farmhouse   showering
his father   holding the urinal
saying later   *I wish I could do more*

It was June   There were bird calls
flickers   robins   certainly Steller's jays
Mt. Jefferson still snow-capped behind the pond

sun glinting in the ripples   an occasional bubble
in the gray surface   A red dragonfly whirred
A *cardinal meadowhawk*   I looked it up

It seemed critical to memorize that name
record every detail   to keep that
in mind   to keep something

# THE VIEWING

On Wednesday at Weddle's Funeral Parlor
I kissed a corpse in a coffin that cost
two thousand six hundred and fifty dollars
and had a nice walnut grain visible on edges
not draped in the American flag.
My brain knew my father-in-law
had been refrigerated. But
the flannel red-checked shirt, suspenders,
jeans looked so normal, I bent to kiss
his brow as though to caress my child:
*Pleasant dreams, sleep tight.*
The stunning bruise of his forehead cold.
I didn't recoil disrespectfully, didn't scream,
*Oh God. Oh God damn.* I wanted no Muzak,
fake flowers, the silk-lined casket displayed
in art gallery light, bowls of Hersheys
and mini Reese's Peanut Butter Cups.
How I missed my New York Jewish family:
mourners who wear black, sit on
hard benches and tear their clothes.

# LEFT FACE

My husband infuriates me
when he saves tape.
*We are not that poor.*

But I am ready to hurl
the damn trash across the linoleum,
leave the marriage
over tape?

Like so much in my life,
it's Dad,
clear lines
across gauze masking
the crater in his cheek:

Tuck Tape, not Scotch
because it clawed less at
radiation-damaged skin.

Such adamant tape:
pieces clinging to gauze
even in the garbage.

Accusatory tape:
*Be nice. I might die soon.*
I was the child he wanted to live for,
but what could I mend?

Mute tape:
the blank white
patch on his cheek
I would never touch.

The smell was like tires in a skid:
Cartons, rolls and rolls from the V.A.,
crowded his closet
already packed

with ancient shoes,
every tie he'd ever worn,
threadbare suits
from Alexander's discounts,

every bottle of scotch
received at Christmas, wrapped
red, green, gold, saved
through my childhood

for that shining day
he'd be Father of the Bride,
supply the wedding liquor,
wouldn't have to pay a dime.

I hate tape,
how it catches on fingers,
on what you try
to repair,

the way it mars a smooth surface
when you have to rip it off,
raw places
it leaves behind.

# ANCESTOR WORSHIP

Cambodians ask about our Easter,
rabbits, eggs,
the Resurrection, of course.
Still, it hangs inside me–
the traditional pogrom:  Cossacks
slaughtering Jews for Lent.

In my classroom, the accents
remind me of my childhood–
*sheina* for beautiful, *dumkopf,*
*kugel:* insults and food.
*Kindela, madela,* the love
we add to any word.

My students tell of crowded boats,
miraculous escape.
We've made that trip.
A seder plate stands for
life–horseradish,
that dark rose with thorns,
another shank bone,
another hard-boiled egg.

Outside it's April.
Wild hyacinth and violets,
deliberate tulips, the sudden
multitudes of red.

My students speak English
with a flavor,
the Last Supper.
Take, eat. Feast
for anniversaries of dying.

We are rice,
grains that cling together,
incense before photos
of our ancestors.

# POTATO IN BOTH WORLDS

Nothing swanky like green pepper
or high class like tomato—
voiceless, colorless,
armless burlap, stinky loam.
This is every day in the *shtetl*—
a Jew grubbing a living.

*Nebach, nothing! You call this*
*a life? Some life!*
How do tubers grow underground?
Somehow, only God knows,
even in Novoroduk
a potato sends out leaves.

So Grandpa Liebowitz,
a shoemaker, goes to America,
contracts with Leake and Watts,
all the soles and heels,
buys real estate. Welcome
to the American dream!

The grandchildren grate potatoes
in the Cuisinart.
No more bloody knuckles.
Add the flour, the salt,
the baking soda, an egg
and the batter will rise.

Onion to make the eyes water
lest we forget.
Fry the *latkes* crisp and brown.
Bite the soft center.
The flavor lingers
in the mouth, in the bone.

# WEBCRAWLER

As if hours of searching
for "Yonkers" and pressing *Enter*
would bring back the Kaminetskys,
Nepperhan Avenue, Terrelli's peaches.
There is a website for Yonkers Police,
and Neal Simon's *Lost in Yonkers*
keeps reappearing.

The screen digitizes the surface
of Yonkers High School:
brick, turrets, steps,
but there is no Mr. Manello,
no band parading Linden Street,
uniforms smelling of mothballs,
the baritone horn I held
blaring.

The Broadway Diner is listed
where we ate lunch every Saturday,
and Mother that final time
sounded out *egg* and *tuna*,
but couldn't say
*lemon meringue pie*

words sticky,
incomprehensible
as dust coating
the tiny pink flowers
on the miniature *limoges* teacup
Uncle David brought back
from the war in Europe,
lost now in Yonkers.

 Lois Rosen lives in Salem, Oregon. She retired from a career of teaching English as a Second Language at Chemeketa Community College. At Willamette University, she co-directed the Advanced Institute of the Oregon Writers' Project. Her poetry has appeared most recently in *Willow Springs, Calyx, Hubbub*, and *Many Mountains Moving*. She has won the Oregon Teachers as Writers Contest, The James de Priest Contest of the Oregon Symphony at Western Oregon University, the Oregon State Poetry Association's Poets' Choice Contest. She graduated from City College of New York with honors in English and from the School for International Training with an M. Ed. in Teaching English as a Second Language.

Particular thanks to the editors who have published my work, my husband, Kevin Davidson, my son, David Rosen, dear family and friends, all my teachers and students, the Oregon Writers' Project at Willamette University, Flight of the Mind, Haystack, the Squaw Valley Community of Writers, the ESL Department at Chemeketa Community College, Annie Callan's Wildheart Writers, and the Peregrine Writers past and present. Deep appreciation to Chris Howell, Nance Van Winckel, Carolyn Miller, Erik Muller, and Carlos Reyes for invaluable advice on the shape of the book, and to Sally Brodigan for the artwork, and Susanlee Graves for the author photo.